Country Cooking

APPLIED ARTS PUBLISHERS

Contents

Recipes

Soups 2
Meat, Fish, Poultry and Eggs 4
Condiments 6
Stuffing and Filling 7
Fritters 8
Vegetables 9
Breads 10
Sandwiches 13
Bread Spreads 14
Pudding 15
Cakes 17
Cake Toppings 18
Cookies 19
Pies 20
Beverages 23
Fruits 26

Cooking 26

The Monday Blues 27

The Applebutter Boiling 28

Baking 29

Gathering 30

Butchering 31

Recipe Index 32

Antiques Index 32

Seventh Printing 1993

LEBANON, PA. 17042

COPYRIGHT 1975, ELMER L. SMITH

ISBN: 0-911410-38-4

Soups

New England Boiled Dinner

In a large kettle, place between four and five pounds of brisket corned beef and enough salted water to cover. Bring to a boil and allow the water to simmer for two to three hours. Skim off the accumulated foam and scum. Add eight medium-sized onions; one medium sized white turnip cut into cubes; eight or ten whole, scraped carrots and allow to simmer for a half hour. Add a cabbage that has been quartered and seven or eight peeled potatoes and enough pepper and salt to season. When the potatoes are tender, drain off the liquid and serve on a large platter. (There are variants to this procedure including the addition of green peas, string beans and other vegetables, but these are more characteristic of a stew, but quite tasty.)

Lentil Soup

Soak one pound of lentils an hour or more; drain and place them in three quarts of boiling water. Dice six slices of bacon and heat over a low flame; dice three carrots; three onions and three stalks of celery and sauté with the bacon. Add a ham bone to the boiling lentils; stir in the bacon and vegetables and cook until the ingredients become a thick consistency. Add the following seasonings to your taste: parsley, thyme, pepper, salt. This makes a hearty meal in itself, with good bread and butter.

(Lentil soup has been called "a mess of pottage" by some folks because lentils were the main ingredient of the famous "mess of pottage" which became Esau's birth right. This dish certainly isn't worth giving up your birthright, but it is worth a try on a cold winter's day!)

Spinach Soup

Strain one cup of cooked spinach into a mash; add four tablespoons of melted butter, two and a half cups of milk and heat slowly. Stir in the liquor from the cooked spinach, a half cup and season with salt and pepper.

(Spinach has been considered a highly nutritious food for many centuries. Mothers for decades have been telling their children, "Eat your spinach and grow up to be big and strong!" Yet all the mothers combined didn't sell spinach as well as *Popeye*.)

Asparagus Soup

Boil asparagus in water (one bunch) and when tender, drain and cut off the tips. Press the asparagus through a seive creating a puree. Mix the puree with three cups of milk; blend in paste made from two tablespoons of flour and two tablespoons of butter and stir constantly bringing the liquid to a boil. Add the asparagus tips and sprinkle salt and pepper to taste. (Some folks sprinkle paprika or grated American cheese on top.)

Cheese Soup

Fry three slices of bacon with two large onions diced. When the onions are tender add three-quarters cup of bread crumbs and three cups of soup stock (bouillon cubes are an adequate substitute). Pepper and salt to taste, and it may be necessary to add butter. Simmer for a half hour with a cover over the skillet. Mix in two ounces of grated American cheese.

Fresh Green Pea Soup

Shell one quart of green garden peas; dice six medium sized onions and place the peas and onions in boiling water to cover. When the vegetables are tender, pour them in a sieve and rub them through making a puree. Add two quarts of milk and return the liquid to a low heat, stirring constantly and blending in two tablespoons of butter and salt and pepper to taste. Serve when the mixture begins to boil. (In earlier days, this soup was served in the summer months when the kitchen garden was at its productive peak.)

Philadelphia Pepper Pot

Wash one pound of tripe carefully, place it in four quarts of boiling water and allow the water to simmer. Peel and slice one medium onion; dice two carrots and add them with the marrow (removed from the bone) and cook together in a skillet until the onions are soft. In the meantime, put a veal knuckle with the marrow bone in a kettle of four quarts of water, boil and then allow it to simmer until the veal is cooked. Cut off the edible veal and discard the bones. Add the contents of the skillet to the veal and its liquid. Add the following seasonings to the tripe that has been simmering: two tablespoons of parsley; two teaspoons of salt, one teaspoon each of black pepper and marjoram; a half teaspoon of allspice and thyme and a dash of red pepper. Add two medium sized potatoes, that have been diced, to the liquid and cook until soft, then combine all ingredients together and before serving add dumpling dough, cover and enjoy! (It has been said that a way to a man's heart is through his stomach, but this recipe is a way to a man's heart through a cow's stomach.)

According to legend, this soup was first made by an army cook at Valley Forge during that harsh winter when the Continental army was both cold and hungry. Regardless, it does have the characteristics of a so-called poverty dish—but it's good!

Cabbage Soup

Chop a young medium sized head of cabbage into small pieces. Boil for a few minutes and remove from heat. Slice and dice a large onion and saute it in three tablespoons of melted butter. When tender mix in one tablespoon of flour and one cup of sour cream and stir constantly. Add three cups of stock or hot water with beef bouillon, then mix in the boiled cabbage that has been drained of liquid. Season with salt and pepper.

Corn Chowder

Peel and dice four cups of potatoes and cook until tender. Slice and dice one large onion and dice a piece of salt pork and fry together for several minutes. Add the onion|salt pork to the potatoes and mix in two cups of corn shredded from the cobs. Stir in a pint of milk and season with salt and pepper.

Tinware was typical of the last century; these light utensils were a welcome replacement for the earlier heavy cast iron and stoneware containers and equipment.

Meat, Fish, Poultry, and Eggs

Lathe turned mortar and pestle of early American vintage. This specimen stands 6-3/4" high.

Shepherd's Pie

Another "left-over" recipe, applicable to those times when a roast leg of lamb has not been entirely consumed, is this simply, easily made dish:

Line a baking dish with left-over mashed potatoes, add a layer of chopped lamb and gravy; add another layer of potatoes and place more lamb and gravy on top; then add a top layer of potatoes. Sprinkle with salt, pepper and dots of butter (some think paprika adds flavor and color!) and bake in a hot oven until the potatoes form a crust.

Rice-Meat Pie

Add four tablespoons of butter, one well-beaten egg and a dash of nutmeg to three cups of boiled rice. Place the ingredients in a baking dash and add leftover meat (cut in small cubes or slices) and gravy and mix it, adding salt and pepper.

Bake in a moderate oven for a half hour.

Simple Stove-Top Supper

Brown a half dozen pork chops in a large frying pan; slice a half dozen medium-sized potatoes and a half-dozen onions and place them in the pan with the chops. Season with salt and pepper then fill the pan with milk, cover and allow the ingredients to simmer until the potatoes are soft and tender. (This is a masculine meal; much appreciated by hard-working men of the "meat-and-potatoes" class.)

Codfish Cakes

Soak two cups of shredded salt codfish overnight in water. In the morning drain and soak the codfish again for an hour or more. Drain and place codfish with four cups of diced raw potatoes and cook until the potatoes are tender.

Beat one egg and mix with two tablespoons of butter and combine with the fish/potato mixture. (Drain off any water first.) Form the ingredients into cakes, sprinkle with pepper and roll in flour and deep fry until golden brown. (Codfish cakes were usually served with stewed tomatoes, some folks used the tomatoes as a sauce over the cakes.)

Liver Loaf

Cook a pound of pork or beef liver in boiling water for ten minutes. Blend one teaspoon of mustard with two teaspoons of water and add it to two cups of bread crumbs or cubes; a finely chopped onion and a half pound of pork sausage. Drain the liver and place it through a grinder and add the liver to the other ingredients. Add half a cup of the liquid in which the liver was cooked, two eggs, one teaspoon of salt and a half teaspoon of black pepper. Form the mixture into a loaf and bake in a greased pan at a moderate temperature.

Red Flannel Hash

Mix together a half dozen beets and an equal amount of potatoes, cooked and chopped or diced and add one cup of chopped cooked corned beef and a half cup of chopped onions.

Fry the ingredients in a large skillet with three tablespoons of butter and season with salt and pepper. Allow the mixture to brown slowly, adding butter when necessary. When a crust forms, serve. (This is a real meat stretcher and serves a good number at a low cost!)

Chicken Croquettes

Grind four cups of chicken or turkey and blend with one tablespoon of chopped parsley and a pint of white sauce (see page 7). Shape this mixture into round balls and cover with bread crumbs that are seasoned with salt and pepper. Dip into beaten eggs, sprinkle with more bread crumbs or cracker crumbs and fry them in deep hot fat until a golden brown. (Chicken was a special Sunday feature on the old-time farm; croquettes were made from the leftover's on Monday.)

Farmers Winter Omelet

Fry six slices of bacon until crisp, remove from the pan. Fry in the bacon grease one medium sliced onion; one cup of potatoes that were boiled and cubed and one half-cup of cubed bread. When the onions are tender add three beaten eggs, three tablespoons of shredded cheddar cheese and salt and pepper to taste, and while the eggs are still moist include the bacon in the mixture and stir.

(This is a real hard-working man's meal, they say it will "stick-to-the-ribs" and it is tasty too! With enough early morning chores, the farmer can work off this healthy breakfast in time for the noonday meal.)

Oblong, market type hand-woven basket measuring 16" long by 12" wide. Few folks expected purchases to be wrapped or placed in a bag—they took their own basket.

Condiments

White Sauce

Melt two tablespoons of butter; blend in two tablespoons of flour and stir in a cup of milk adding salt and pepper to taste. This makes a sauce of medium thickness, to make a thin liquid reduce the quantity of flour; to make a heavy, thick sauce increase the amount of flour. (Other variants include the addition of a quantity of dried mustard; grated American cheese; finely chopped onions; thin slices of green pepper or chopped pimiento.)

Lemon Sauce

Blend together a tablespoon of cornstarch, a half teaspoon of salt and a half cup of sugar with a quarter cup of cold water. Stir in three-quarters cup of boiling water and maintain heat until the mixture is thick. Combine the yolk of an egg with three tablespoons of lemon juice and stir into the thickening mixture. Add one teaspoon of grated lemon rind, two tablespoons of butter and a sprinkling of nutmeg and stir one minute before removing the sauce from the heat.

This sauce is very good on gingerbread, steamed puddings, fruit puddings and fruit cake.

Mustard Dressing

Mix one teaspoon of powdered mustard with two teaspoons of water and allow to stand. Blend together two tablespoons of flour, one tablespoon of sugar and a teaspoon of salt. Beat the yolks of two eggs and add three quarters cup of water and blend in with the mustard liquid and the dry ingredients. Cook over hot water, in a double boiler, until the sauce is thick. Stir in a quarter cup of vinegar and two tablespoons of salad oil.

This is particularly good with cabbage, cooked or in slaw and over vegetable salads.

Hot Dressing for Greens

Fry five slices of bacon, drain on absorbent paper. Add a half cup of milk to the bacon fat. Mix two beaten eggs with salt, four tablespoons of vinegar and two tablespoons of brown sugar. Combine with the milk in the skillet and continue stirring until the mixture thickens. Remove from the heat and sprinkle with pepper and pour over the greens. Crush the bacon slices and sprinkle it on top of each serving.

Nutmeg Sauce

Combine one cup of sugar with three tablespoons of flour, a dash of salt and a quarter teaspoon of nutmeg and stir in two cups of boiling water. Cook until the mixture thickens. Add a tablespoon of butter and a tablespoon of vinegar and stir carefully as the product is being removed from the stove. (This is good on apple dishes, particularly on apple dumplings and baked apples.)

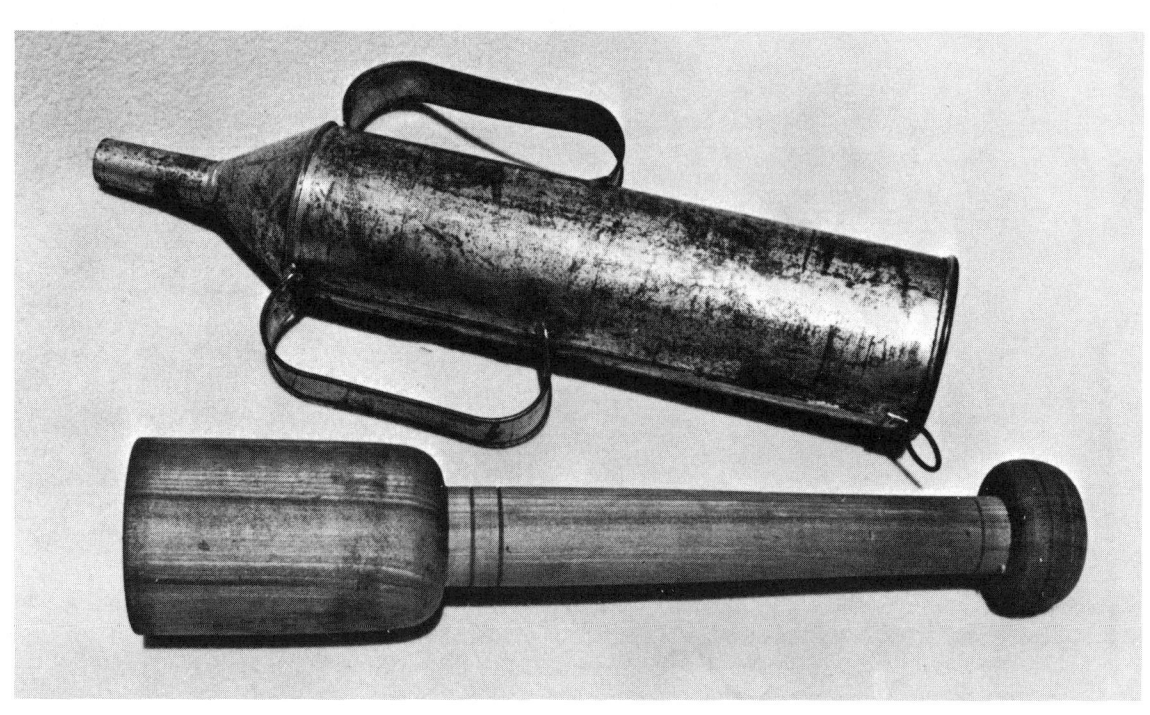

Large tin sausage stuffer with wooden press, 19" long. The typical tin stuffer was 12" in size and most of these were replaced by the heavy duty iron stuffers available after mid-century.

Stuffing and Filling

Sausage Stuffing

Blend together a half pound of sausage meat, two cups of bread crumbs and one medium sized onion chopped fine. Add one tablespoon of minced parsley, a half teaspoon of pepper and salt. This may be stuffed inside a small turkey, chicken or baked separately. (It is a contrast with poultry, but some folks make it as a main part of the meal as a separate dish!)

Corn Bread Filling

Blend together three cups of crumbled corn bread; three cups of stale bread cubes; one cup of chopped celery; one medium sized onion, minced; a half tablespoon of poultry seasoning two teaspoons of salt and enough melted butter to moisten. This recipe makes enough for a small turkey.

Sage Stuffing

Melt a cup of butter in a skillet, add one cup of chopped onions, a half cup of chopped celery, and two tablespoons of chopped parsley and simmer until tender. Add three quarts of toasted bread cubes, pepper, salt and enough chicken stock or broth to moisten. Crumble dried sage leaves into the stuffing (three teaspoons or more) and mix carefully. This should fill a 16-pound turkey.

Oyster Stuffing

Follow the directions and ingredients for the Sage Stuffing but replace the chicken broth with oyster liquor and add a cup and a half of chopped drained oysters.

Hand-made, wooden bench type lard press, stands 36" high.

Apple Dressing

Melt six tablespoons of butter and mix in three cups of cubed bread slices; four cups of diced apples; one cup of chopped celery, three tablespoons of chopped parsley and a pinch of salt, pepper and nutmeg. Stuff inside poultry or bake separately.

Bread Stuffing

Mix together three cups of bread crumbs and two cups of toasted bread cubes, add one medium size onion chopped fine; one cup of chopped celery, two well beaten eggs, a half teaspoon of sage; salt and pepper and enough milk to moisten the ingredients.

Orange Dressing

Orange stuffing is popular when roasting either goose or duck. The following ingredients should fill a ten pound goose:
    8 cups of toasted bread crumbs
    ¾ cup of chopped celery
    ¾ cup of chopped onions
    2 cups of diced oranges
    ½ cup of poultry stock or chicken bouillion broth.

Combine all the above ingredients, add 2 teaspoons of salt; two of ground thyme; two of grated orange rind and a half teaspoon of pepper and mix well. Insert the stuffing in the neck and body of the goose. (If a duck is to be roasted, about half the quantities should be sufficient.)

Fritters

Fritters

Cheese-Potato Fritters

Mix together a quarter cup of cold mashed potatoes and a similar amount of grated American cheddar cheese. Add a half onion, chopped fine and two beaten eggs with salt and pepper to taste. Drop by the spoonful into deep hot fat and fry until golden brown. Drain on an absorbent paper and serve.

Corn Fritters

Shred the kernels from enough ears of fresh corn to make a pint of pulp. Mix the corn with three beaten eggs, three tablespoons of cream and four tablespoons of flour to make a thin paste. Drop the mixture into hot fat a spoonful at a time. Fry until they are a crisp golden brown.

The lard press was once a common farmstead implement. Such hand-equipment was often made of hardwood—those shown are from oak, walnut and yellow pine, and are from Virginia, Maryland and West Virginia.

Eggplant Fritters

Peel, slice and boil an eggplant in salted water. Mash the eggplant as you do in making mashed potatoes, then mix in two beaten eggs; two teaspoons of baking powder, one tablespoon of sugar and flour enough to make a thick batter. A spoonful at a time of this mixture should be dropped into a hot, well buttered frying pan. Brown on both sides.

Peach Fritters

Follow the same procedure as in making the Corn Fritters (below) except fresh ripe peaches are mashed and substituted for the corn. This dish was served with the main meal, not as a dessert, they were a delicious addition to summer meals on the farm in years gone by.

Banana Fritters

Aunt Sarah made four fritters from one banana. She halved, cut lengthwise and then cut crosswise, and allowed the bananas to stand a quarter hour in a dish with lemon juice squeezed over them. She then made her "fritter batter" and when she was ready to fry, she took a tablespoonful of the batter with a slice of banana for each fritter, dropped it into hot fat until it was brown then sifted pulverized sugar over it and served it hot.

Fritter Batter

Sift together one pint of flour, two teaspoons of baking powder and a pinch of salt. Stir slowly into a pint of milk, add yolks of three beaten eggs and finally add the stiffly beaten whites of eggs.

Wooden, hand-made press, 31" long, was used in the days when preserving food for the winter larder was a major summer and fall seasonal task.

Vegetables

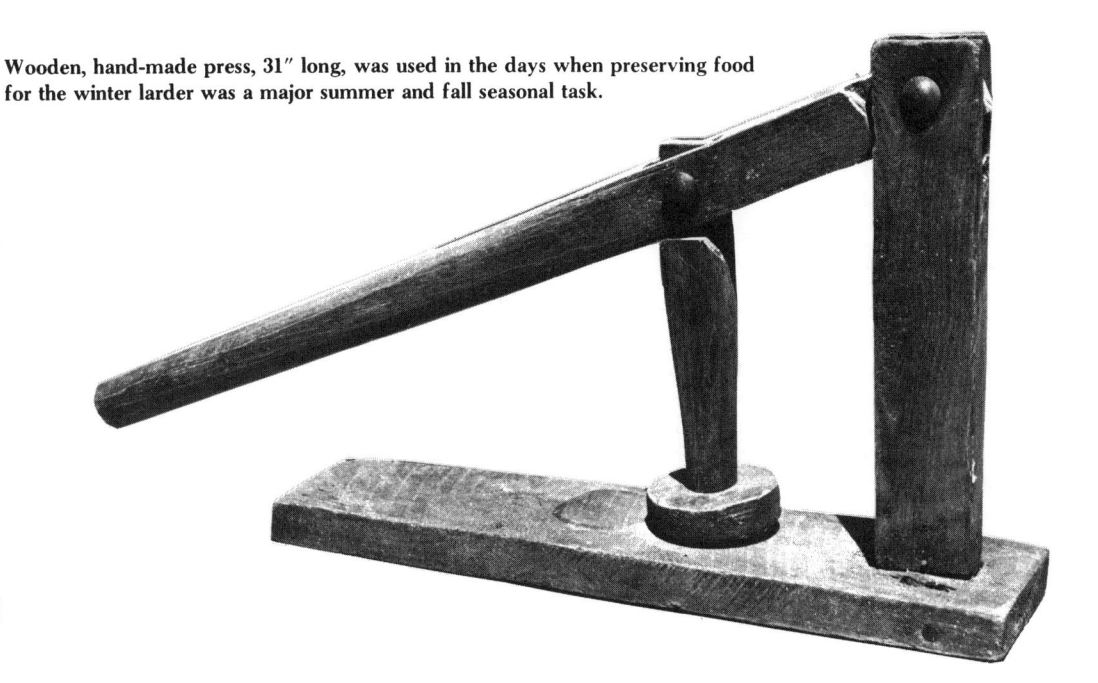

Onion Greens

Chop the green tops from 20 or 30 spring onions, cook in boiling water until they are tender. Drain and chop them fine. In a heavy frying pan melt three tablespoons of butter or bacon fat, add the onion greens and sprinkle them with salt and pepper. Fry until they are brown.

Deep Fried Parsnips

Boil parsnips in salted water until they are tender. Remove the skins and cut them into half-inch slices. Roll the slices in flour which has been seasoned with salt and pepper, fry them in deep hot fat until crisp and brown. Drain and serve. (Country folks usually deep fry left-over parsnips, at first serving it is most common to boil parsnips and serve them skinned, sliced and buttered.)

Beet Greens

Wash the tops of beets several times or they may be gritty. Place the greens in a deep pan, sprinkle with salt and add a small quantity of water. Cover and boil until they are tender. Serve hot with a large piece of butter on top. (Have a cruet of vinegar on the table, many people who enjoy greens sprinkle cider vinegar on them.)

Scalloped Potatoes

Cut a quart of raw potatoes into quarter-inch slices, place in a well-buttered casserole, and season each layer with salt, pepper and dabs of butter. Pour over this two cups of white sauce (see page 7) and bake in a moderate oven for about an hour.

Creamed Spinach

Melt three tablespoons of butter in a pan and blend in two tablespoons of flour. Add a cup of milk and cook over low heat. Stir in two cups of chopped cooked spinach and season with salt and pepper. The dish is ready to serve when the ingredients form a thick paste like consistency.

Baked Beans

Soak one quart of dried navy beans overnight in cold water. Drain, cover with boiling water and cook until the skins burst. Place one chopped onion in the bean pot, add a tablespoon of mustard; three tablespoons of molasses and three tablespoons of brown sugar and pour in a cup of boiling salted water. Drain the beans of water, pour into the bean pot and add cubed salted pork on top. Cover the pot and bake slowly (adding water if needed from time to time) and remove the cover one hour before serving, this allows the beans to brown.

Potato-Onion Cakes

To a pint of mashed potatoes blend in two beaten eggs and three tablespoons of milk; season with diced onions and salt and pepper. Form the mixture into small cakes and fry until brown on both sides in hot bacon fat.

Chicken-Potato Puffs

Grind three cups of leftover chicken in a food chopper. Mix in with a cup and a half of mashed potatoes and two tablespoons of minced parsely and season with salt and pepper. Roll the ingredients into balls (the size of golf balls) and brush with melted butter and roll them in cracker crumbs or bread crumbs. These may be fried in deep fat until brown or baked in a greased casserole dish in a moderate oven.

Potato-Cheese Cakes

Follow the same procedure as in making Potato-Onion cakes but add to the mixture a good quantity of grated American cheese. (A variation of this is to fry the potato cakes, then remove them and place the cheese on the top of each cake and place the fry pan under the broiler heat until the cheese melts and bubbles!)

Breads

Fried Corn Mush

Bring three cups of water and one cup of milk mixed together to a boiling point. Mix one tablespoon of sugar, two teaspoons of salt, one tablespoon of flour and one cup of corn meal and gradually blend it in with the liquid. Cook until the ingredients thicken and place over hot water in a double boiler and continue cooking for 30-45 minutes.

Pour into a loaf pan and let the mixture cool overnight. In the morning cut it into slices and fry in hot fat until brown on both sides. Serve it hot with maple syrup. (Some folks just cover it with butter and sprinkle salt and pepper over it. Mothers will usually find that children who will not want to eat corn meal mush will eat this!)

Cranberry Muffins

Cream a quarter cup of butter with the same amount of brown sugar and a beaten egg. Mix together the following dry ingredients; two cups of sifted flour; three teaspoons of baking powder; a half teaspoon of salt and a dash of nutmeg. Combine the mixtures and dampen with enough milk to make a thick dough—about one cup. Stir in one cup of chopped raw cranberries and a teaspoon of flavoring (orange or vanilla are both good!). Bake in greased muffin tins in a hot oven.

Huckleberry Muffins

Sift two cups of flour, two teaspoons of baking powder, a half teaspoon of salt and five tablespoons of sugar into a mixing bowl. Add one cup of milk, one beaten egg, three heaping tablespoons of butter (melted) and fold in one and a half cups of huckleberries. Pour into well greased muffin tins and bake in a hot oven until they are a golden brown.

Peanut Muffins

Chop a half cup of peanuts very fine; add two cups of flour and three teaspoons of baking powder and mix in one egg, a half cup of sugar and a half cup of milk adding a dash of salt. Mix well and place a spoonful of the batter in each section of a well-buttered muffin pan. Bake about a half hour in a moderate oven.

Buttermilk Doughnuts

Flour (2 cups)	Shortening (3 tablespoons)
Egg (one)	Baking Powder (½ teaspoon)
Sugar (½ cup)	Soda (½ teaspoon)
Buttermilk (½ cup)	Nutmeg (a sprinkling)
	Salt (½ teaspoon)

Combine one beaten egg with a half cup of sugar and melted shortening, mix in the buttermilk. Add flour; baking powder, soda, nutmeg and salt mixing carefully. Roll the dough on a floured board and cut out the two dozen or so doughnuts. Fry in deep fat at 375°—turning each when they reach that golden brown color. Remove and place on an absorbent paper to drain and cool.

An ingenious wooden cabbage cutting device—pump the handle and the cutter blade is raised and lowered against the cabbage in the box. Cabbage was a common dish, perhaps because it stored well over a long period of time. Most farms had slaw or cabbage cutting devices in a variety of types and sizes.

Crullers

Cut a half pound of butter into two pounds of sifted flour, add three quarters of a pound of sugar, a teaspoon of nutmeg; a teaspoon of cinnamon and mix well. Beat six eggs and pour them in the batter along with two tablespoons of milk. Knead the dough carefully. Roll the dough on a floured board and cut in narrow strips a half inch thick. Twist the strips and place them in hot fat, turning them when brown on one side. Remove and drain on absorbent paper. Sprinkle with powdered sugar. (Although we presently associate doughnuts with dunking, I believe crullers were the most likely to have originally found their way inside a cup of coffee.)

Shortcake Biscuits

Flour (3 cups)	Cream of Tartar (2 teaspoons)
Salt (½ teaspoon)	Shortening (6 tablespoons)
Soda (1¼ teaspoon)	Milk (1½ cups)

Sift all the dry ingredients together; add shortening and blend; stir in milk until you have a soft dough. Roll the dough, using a biscuit cutter, press out the dozen and a half this recipe makes. (Granny used to cut the biscuits with a tea cup, they were much larger than usual and very appropriate for individual strawberry shortcake servings!) Bake in a preheated oven at 450° for a quarter of an hour.

Milk Biscuits

Cut a quarter pound of butter into a pound of sifted flour, add a pint and a half of milk and stir. Beat two eggs and combine with the dough then add yeast and mix carefully.

Flour the board, knead the dough and cut into small pieces and knead them into round balls. Pierce the top of each with a fork. Place them on buttered pans and set them to rise. (About an hour in a warm place.) Bake in a moderate oven.

Cabbage cutter, 16″ square, made to fit over a barrel or large crock. The cylinder crank rotates blades which shred the cabbage. (Most "kraut" cutters were simple boards with a metal blade).

Maryland Beaten Biscuit

Flour (4 cups)	Butter (or Lard) ½ cup
Milk (½ cup)	Water (½ cup)
Salt (1 teaspoon)	Sugar (1 tablespoon)
Baking Powder (1 teaspoon)	

Mix the dry ingredients together; cut the lard into the mixture and add the milk and water blending to create a stiff dough. Fold and knead this dough until it is smooth and elastic in quality. Roll the dough on a floured board to half-inch thickness, cut into two inch rounds. Grease a baking sheet with butter; place biscuit on the sheet; insert a fork in each and brush with melted butter. Bake in a medium heat. This recipe makes about a dozen and a half. (Some of my friends form these biscuits into spheres, or fold them in half. This is unusually good with country ham or cheddar cheese inserted between the folds!)

Sweet Dough

Dissolve two yeast cakes in warm water; add a quarter cup of lard, a half cup of sugar, a teaspoon of salt and a cup of milk. Mix in two beaten eggs, two teaspoons of grated rind of a lemon and enough flour to make a soft dough (about 4 to 5 cups). When the dough is well mixed, place it on a floured board and knead it until it has a satiny, shiny appearance. Place it in a greased bowl, cover it and let it rise until it doubles in bulk. Press or knead it back down, shape the dough into whatever form it is to be (loaves, cakes, rings, rolls, or twists) and let it rise again. Bake at 375°.

Pineapple or Strawberry Buns

Roll the **Sweet Dough** to a quarter inch thickness, cut with a 3" round cookie cutter and place half of them on a greased baking sheet. Cut holes in the centers of the remaining rounds and remove the dough, then place these over the other rounds. Fill the centers with pineapple or strawberry jam. Let the dough rise until it doubles and bake for a quarter hour at 375°.

(The filling can be made in a variety of ways: chopped nuts; brown sugar and raisins; lemon-cornstarch filling; or any jams, blackberry, peach or plum are very good.)

Cinnamon Loaf

When the **Sweet Dough** is light, place it in a greased rectangular cake pan, drop small pieces of butter on top, sprinkle generously with dark brown sugar and dashes of cinnamon and a pinch of nutmeg. Let the dough rise until double in bulk and bake at 375° for a quarter of an hour.

Whole Wheat Bread

In a half cup of warm water add two packages of dry yeast and stir to dissolve. Mix together a cup and a half of water, two tablespoons of brown sugar, one tablespoon of salt, one tablespoon of melted lard and blend in three cups of whole wheat flour and stir in the yeast and mix until it is a smooth batter. Mix in two or three cups of flour a little at a time until the dough is stiff. Place the dough on a floured board and knead it. Round up the dough and place it in a greased bowl and cover it with a dry cloth and let it rise until it is about double in bulk. Punch it down, divide the dough into two loaves and cover them again and let the dough rise (a quarter of an hour should be long enough). Shape the loaves and put them in greased pans. Cover and wait until the dough doubles in bulk then bake in a moderate oven at 375° for an hour or slightly less.

Bran Bread

Dissolve one yeast cake in a cup of lukewarm milk. Combine one cup of all-bran cereal in one and a half cups of water and boil. Add a half cup of shortening, three tablespoons of sugar, two teaspoons of salt and six cups of flour. Knead, let it rise two hours in a warm place. Divide dough into loaves; let them rise again, an hour or more. Bake at 375° for three-quarters of an hour or more.

Pine, dove-tailed candle box, measures 12" long. Most early American homes made their own supply of candles from tallow, bees wax or bayberry leaves—it was simply another of the many kitchen chores of the past.

Sandwiches

Peanut Butter and Bacon Sandwich

Fry three slices of bacon for each sandwich until crisp. Remove, drain and crumble the bacon. Spread a liberal amount of peanut butter on a slice of bread, then sprinkle the bacon over it and add the top slice of bread. Very tasty.

(Remember the old style, hand-ground peanut butter you bought by the pound at the open market? That was before homogenization; it stuck to the roof of your mouth!)

Egg-Cheese Sandwich

Chop two hard-cooked eggs and blend them with three tablespoons of mayonnaise, mix in two tablespoons of grated American cheddar cheese and season with salt and pepper. Spread on buttered slices of bread.

Onion-Cheese Sandwich

Mix together one cup of American cheddar cheese with a half cup of finely chopped onions run through a grinder (include the onion juice!) and add two tablespoons of finely chopped green peppers, a teaspoon of mustard and three tablespoons of mayonnaise. This makes a very tasty spread. (Two variants are noteworthy: the spread is enhanced by the addition of thin slices of ham or thin slices of fresh tomato!)

The mixture is quite moist and sandwiches made up too long before serving may become soggy. Keep the mixture refrigerated until immediately prior to its use.

Bean Sandwich

Left-over baked beans make a tasty sandwich! Mash two cups of beans and mix in two tablespoons of mayonnaise, one tablespoon of finely chopped onions; one tablespoon of chopped sweet pickle or chili sauce and a few drops of cider vinegar. Spread liberally on buttered bread.

Liverwurst and Bacon Sandwich

Fry six slices of bacon until crisp. Remove from skillet and drain. Crumble the bacon and blend with six tablespoons of liverwurst; adding two tablespoons of mayonnaise and one teaspoon of prepared mustard (some folks might prefer catsup!) and one teaspoon of finely chopped onion. Spread on bread. Rye or whole wheat bread is particularly good with this spread.

Chopped Meat Sandwich

Force one pound of left-over pork, beef, or both through a meat grinder and add two tablespoons of finely chopped onion, two tablespoons of chopped green peppers and one tablespoon of catsup and four tablespoons of mayonnaise, mixing carefully. Spread on slices of bread. This is extra good with rye or pumpernickle!

Cucumber-Chive Sandwich

Chop a medium sized cucumber in fine pieces and soak in cold water. Drain and add one tablespoon of minced chives and salt and pepper. Mix in one teaspoon of minced parsley flakes and three tablespoons of mayonnaise.

Spread the mixture on white bread. (This is almost exclusively recommended by the disstaff side; the men folk are much more likely to reach for that bean sandwich!)

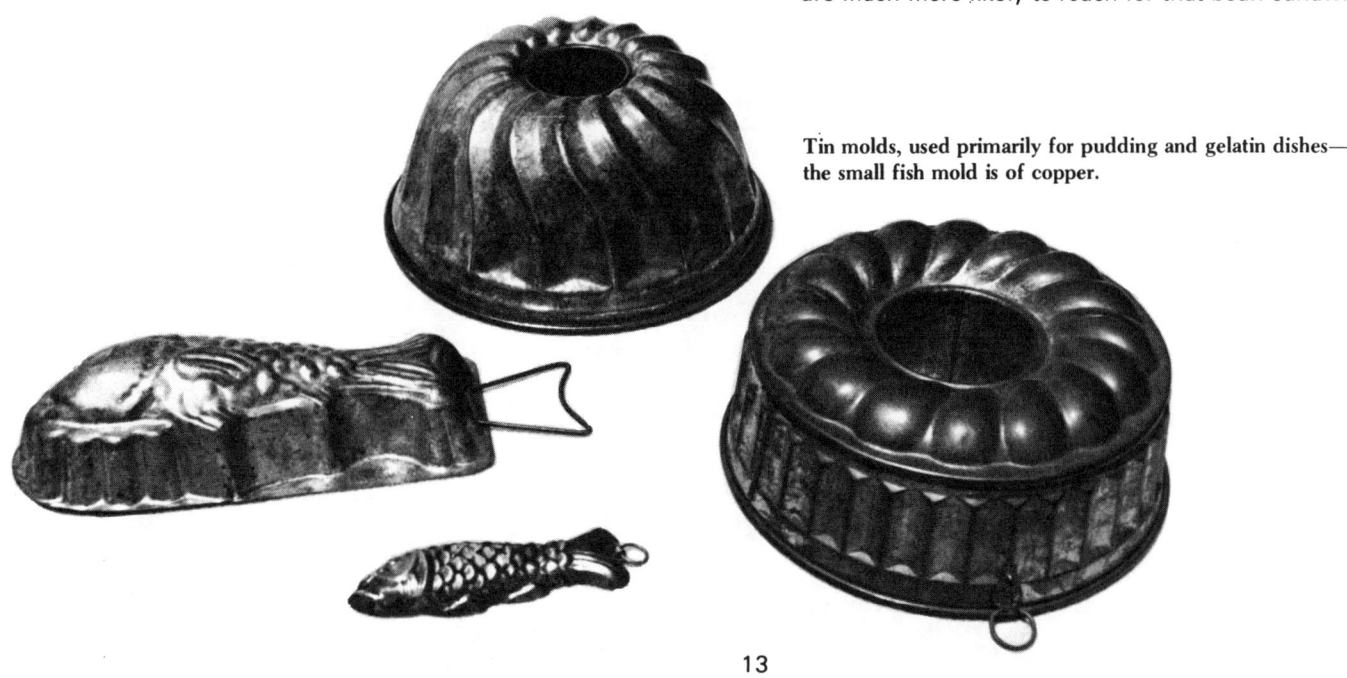

Tin molds, used primarily for pudding and gelatin dishes—
the small fish mold is of copper.

Bread Spreads

Applebutter

Wash, pare, and quarter twelve pounds of apples. Boil seven quarts of cider for a half hour then add the apples and cook until tender. Press the apples through a collander and add eight cups of sugar; three tablespoons of cinnamon; two tablespoons each of ground cloves and allspice and cook until the mixture becomes a soft paste. Stir consistently to avoid scorching and pour into heated jars and seal.

This modern version uses sugar and much less time, yet offers a reasonable likeness to the old-time variety which kept for years without sealing. (One brief observation, why not use some root of sassafras in the boiling mixture, it offers a distinctive flavor.)

Candied Orange Peel

Cut orange peel in thin narrow strips about two inches long. Cover with cold water and bring to a boil and cook for half a hour. Pour off the water, cover with cold water again and boil for a quarter of an hour and drain. Add an equal amount of sugar to peels and simmer over low heat for an hour. Dip peel slices in granulated sugar.

They make a nice treat as a candy for those with a sweet tooth, but they can also be diced and used as ingredients in baking such items as fruit cake or in minced meat as "stretchers." (A similar process can be used to make candied grapefruit, lemon, or lime peel.)

Cheese and Bread

Combine three tablespoons of butter and one teaspoon of mustard to make a spread for five or six slices of bread. Cut the bread into strips and place them in a baking dish. Mix together three beaten eggs and a cup and a half of milk and pour it over the slices of bread. Sprinkle over the top a half pound of grated Cheddar cheese and salt and pepper to season. Bake in a medium oven until the top is a light brown.

Rhubarb Marmalade

Dice two pounds of rhubarb and cover with two pounds of sugar and let it stand overnight. The next morning, add the juice of one orange and a half lemon. Grind the rinds of the orange and half of a lemon and add it to the mixture. Cook for one or two hours until the liquid thickens. Pour into jars and seal.

Rhubarb Jam

Skin and cut three pounds of rhubarb into half-inch pieces. Add two pounds of granulated sugar and a half cup of water and bring to a boil. Add the juice of two oranges and grate the rind of one orange and blend it into the mixture. Stir enough to prevent scorching—a half hour of boiling should make it appear clean. This makes a very good jam. (Some folks add a half cup of seedless raisins to the ingredients.)

New England maple sugar water bucket made of copper and brass. The tin sugar water dipper is from a camp in Somerset County, Pennsylvania.

Pudding

Peach Pudding

Combine a teaspoon of vanilla, three tablespoons of butter, a half cup of sugar, the yolks of two eggs and the rind of one lemon grated and carefully mixed. Sift in a cup of flour, five dashes of salt, three teaspoons of baking powder and gradually stir in a half cup of milk.

Butter a large baking dish and fill it with a dozen peeled and sliced ripe peaches. Dash a sprinkling of lemon juice over the peaches and sprinkle a half cup of sugar over the fruit. Pour the prepared mixture over the fruit and bake it for a half an hour in a medium hot oven.

While the pudding is baking prepare a meringue from the egg whites and sugar and place this on the baking pudding. Add a dusting of either nutmeg or cinnamon. When the topping is brown it is ready to serve. (In the open country folks liked to pour rich, thick creamy milk over it, but now-a-days, perhaps that's asking for too much!)

Indian Pudding

Heat a pint of milk and a pint of molasses, stirring constantly. Beat four eggs and gradually stir them into the liquid mixture. Chop a pound of beef suet very fine and mix it with a quart of corn meal; then gradually stir this into the liquid. Add a teaspoon of cinnamon and one teaspoon of nutmeg and the grated rind from an orange or lemon.

Dip a fine woven cloth in boiling water, wring it out and flour the cloth, pour the mixture in it and tie it up. Place the bag in boiling water—leaving enough room for the pudding to expand and swell up—after three hours, serve it hot with a favorite sauce.

(Any leftovers were cut in slices and fried—some folks liked it better the second day especially when maple syrup was available to pour over it!)

Sugar chest, common to the Southland, measures 21" by 18" and had a lock and butterfly hinges. The lock, so often found on such containers, reflects the high price of refined commercial sugar in earlier times and the tendency to use it sparingly.

Bread Pudding

Line two cups of stale bread cubes and crumbs in a baking dish. Pour two cups of warm milk over the bread, cover and allow the liquid to be absorbed into the bread, add the yolks of two eggs, salt, a tablespoon of sugar and the grated rind of one lemon. (Or a teaspoon of vanilla extract may be added to the warm milk.) Add two stiffly beaten egg whites and stir the entire mixture. Bake in a moderate oven. This was usually served hot with a cold sauce poured over it (see page 7).

Apple Johnny Pudding

Mix together one cup of corn meal, one cup of sour milk, two-thirds cup of flour, two tablespoons of sugar, one tablespoon of melted butter and one teaspoon of soda and a dash of salt. Pare, chore, and thinly slice four apples and add them to the batter. Bake in a hot oven, serve hot with cream and sugar.

Sweet Potato Pudding

Boil and peel a quarter pound of sweet potatoes, mash them until they are smooth, then rub the potato mash through a sieve. Stir a quarter pound of powdered sugar and a quarter pound of butter; add three beaten eggs and combine all ingredients together, thin by adding a wine glass of brandy and a wine glass of milk. Stir in a small quantity of mace, nutmeg and cinnamon. Place the mixture in a plate well buttered and bake half an hour.

Raisin-Rice Pudding

Soak two tablespoons of rice for a half hour. Mix together one cup of raisins, a quarter cup of sugar, one quart of milk, and a teaspoon of vanilla extract and place in a buttered baking dish. Add the drained rice and a quarter teaspoon each of salt, nutmeg and cinnamon and bake in a slow oven until the pudding is firm and the top is browned. (It helps to stir every half hour or so while it is baking.)

Huckleberry picker, this ingenious yellow-pine hand-made device was carried on berry picking jaunts in the mountains of West Virginia. The box measures 13" and has a leather handle.

Cakes

Gingerbread

Mix a half pound of butter into one and a half cups of sifted flour. Add a half cup of ginger. Stir a dash of soda in vinegar (less than a teaspoon) and add it to a half pint of milk and a half pint of molasses. Stir the ingredients together for a long time. Knead it.

On a floured dough board, curl up the dough into round cakes (or straight lengths as in making crullers) and place them in buttered pans. The individual rolls may touch each other. Bake in a moderate oven. (Some women simply bake the dough in large square or oblong tins and cut the cake into squares after it is baked).

Clove Cake

Place one cup of water in a cooking pan, add a cup of brown sugar and two cups of seedless raisins; mix in a third cup of lard or shortening, two teaspoons of cinnamon and a half teaspoon each of ground cloves and ground nutmeg adding a dash of salt. Bring to a boil and cook for five minutes then allow the mixture to cool. Dissolve one teaspoon of soda in a small amount of hot water and add to the cooling mixture—blend in one and three-quarter cups of sifted flour and a half teaspoon of baking powder. Bake in a moderate oven for a half hour.

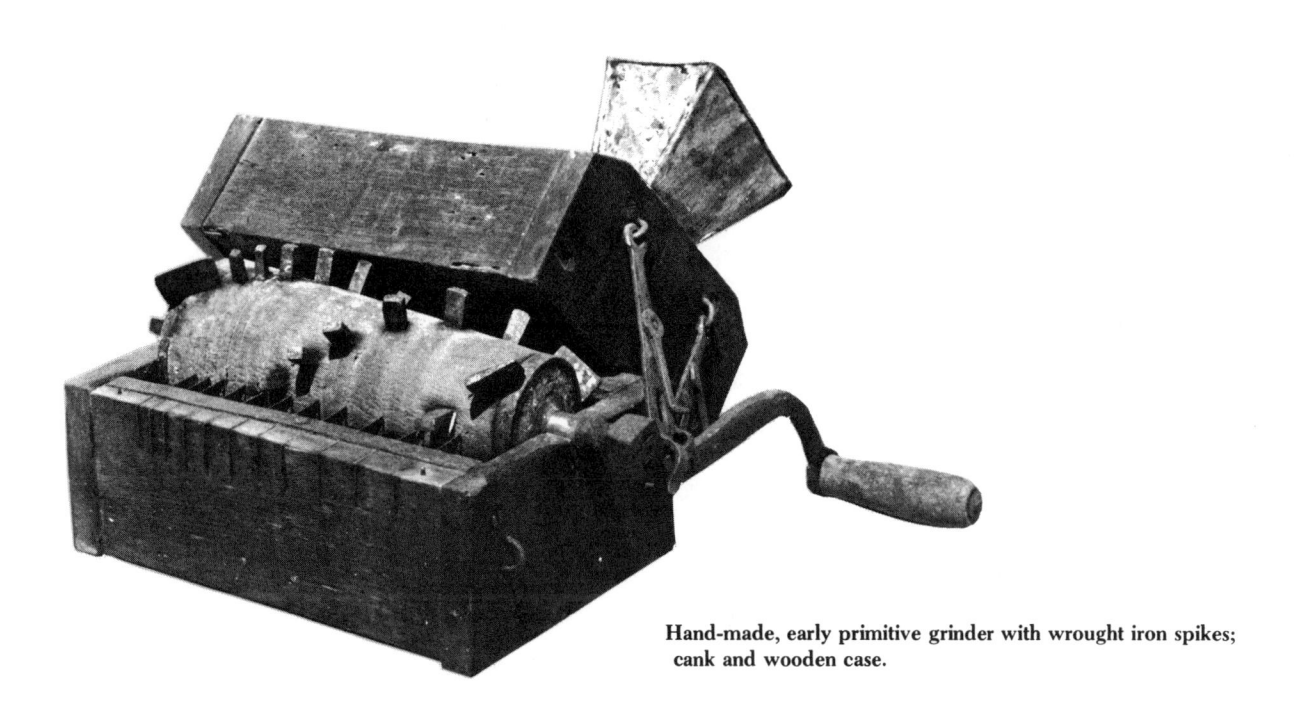

Hand-made, early primitive grinder with wrought iron spikes; cank and wooden case.

Ginger Cake

Stir a half cup of brown sugar and a half cup of lard to a cream. Beat in two cups of flour and set the mixture aside. Dissolve one teaspoon of soda in a half cup of warm water, pour into the mixture adding one tablespoon of ginger. Combine the ingredients and add the white of one egg (beaten), stir carefully and pour the batter into well-buttered baking tins and bake in a hot oven for three-quarters of an hour.

Squash Cake

Combine together one cup of brown sugar or dark molasses, one cup of white sugar, a half cup of butter and one cup of cooked yellow squash and beat until smooth. Sift together and into the beaten mixture the following dry ingredients: three cups of flour; four teaspoons of baking powder; a quarter teaspoon of baking soda; beat in a half cup of milk; one teaspoon of lemon flavoring and one teaspoon of vanilla extract. Pour in a large greased loaf pan and bake in a moderate oven a half hour or more. (A plain icing is recommended.)

Cake Toppings

Golden (Lemon) Sauce

Grandma baked so often that sometimes one of her least popular cakes, or one of her occasional mistakes, went stale. Soon after such an experience we would have a dessert referred to only as "Golden Sauce Cake." Actually it was nothing more than a tasty sauce that was placed directly over the stale-left-over-cake but *that* was never openly admitted! Here is how to make that culinary manipulation sauce: Blend together a half teaspoon of salt; one tablespoon of cornstarch; a half cup of sugar with a quarter cup of cold water. Stir in three-fourths cup of boiling water and continue stirring it over medium heat until the mixture is clean and thickening. Mix an egg yolk with three tablespoons of lemon juice and stir it into the heating sauce. Add one teaspoon of grated lemon rind; four dashes of ground nutmeg and two tablespoons of butter and stir well for one minute. Serve this over slices of cake. (In addition to being used as a "mask," it is very good as a sauce on gingerbread, steamed puddings and left-overs such as bread pudding.)

Honey Frosting

Combine the white of one egg with three tablespoons of white sugar, two tablespoons of water, a dash of salt and a third of a cup of honey in the top of a double boiler. As the mixture heats, mix it with a hand rotary beater until the mixture forms peaks. Add one teaspoon of lemon extract and half as much vanilla flavoring and beat briefly, it is ready for use as a cake topping. (Try it on a spicy gingerbread or apple sauce cake.)

Maple-Nut Icing

Boil together two cups of maple sugar (or syrup) a dash of salt and a cup of milk and allow it to cook until it passes the standard test (a small amount of the heated liquid should form a soft ball when dropped in cold water). Pour the ingredients into a bowl and beat rapidly as it cools. Add a half cup of finely chopped walnuts, a half teaspoon of cinnamon and spread it over a layer cake.

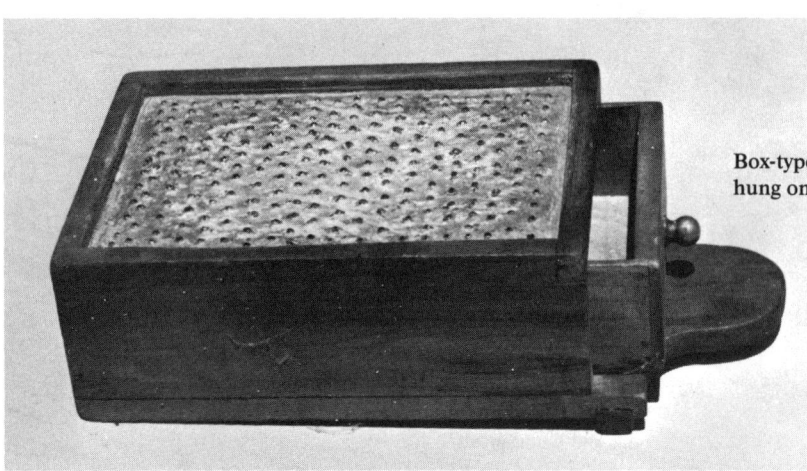

Box-type cheese grater has removable wooden drawer. Can be hung on the kitchen wall when not in use.

Mocha Icing

An Amish housewife made the fastest icing I ever saw, and she did it without measuring a single ingredient! While folks were talking and visiting in "her" kitchen, she mixed together some powdered cocoa; powdered sugar and a lump of butter and creamed them, adding a quantity of hot coffee from the stove. In minutes she spread it between the layers of vanilla cake and casually covered the top and sides, she placed the cake on the table and poured the same coffee (that had been brewing on the kitchen wood stove) and offered everyone refreshments.

Later, I asked her what she called that frosting and she said, "I think of it as *hurry-up* icing, but it is also called *Mocha.*"

Cookies

Raisin Drops

Boil two and a half cups of raisins in one cup of water for five minutes or more. Stir in one teaspoon of baking soda and allow the ingredients to cool. Cream one cup of butter with two cups of sugar, add three beaten eggs and one teaspoon each of vanilla extract and lemon flavoring and add it to the cooling raisins.

Sift together four cups of flour; 1½ teaspoons of baking powder; ½ teaspoon of salt; 1 teaspoon of cinnamon; ¼ teaspoon each of nutmeg and allspice and blend these dry ingredients into the other mixture.

Drop the dough by teaspoonfuls on greased cookie sheets allowing space for them to spread out. Bake at 425° until nicely browned.

When these are cool, store in a tightly covered container to keep them soft. (Some folks add chopped nuts to this batter; if that is your preference, use one cup.)

Nutmeg Wafers

Sift two cups of flour with two teaspoons of baking powder and a half teaspooon of salt. Blend one cup of sugar with three-fourths teaspoon of ground nutmeg, one and a half teaspoons of vanilla extract and two-thirds cup of butter. Add one beaten egg and gradually blend in the flour. Add one cup of milk gradually to moisten.

Preheat the oven to moderate temperature. Drop teaspoonful of dough on an ungreased cookie sheet allowing room for the dough to spread—if necessary press the dough down into a 1/16th of an inch thickness. Bake until they are brown around the edges and when cool, store in airtight containers.

(It is the better part of wisdom to make enough for two batches, the ingredients above make about fifty two-inch cookies. Mom used to wonder what happened to the first sheet of cookies that came from the oven—her children usually admitted that they "tested" one or two but that was always an understatement!)

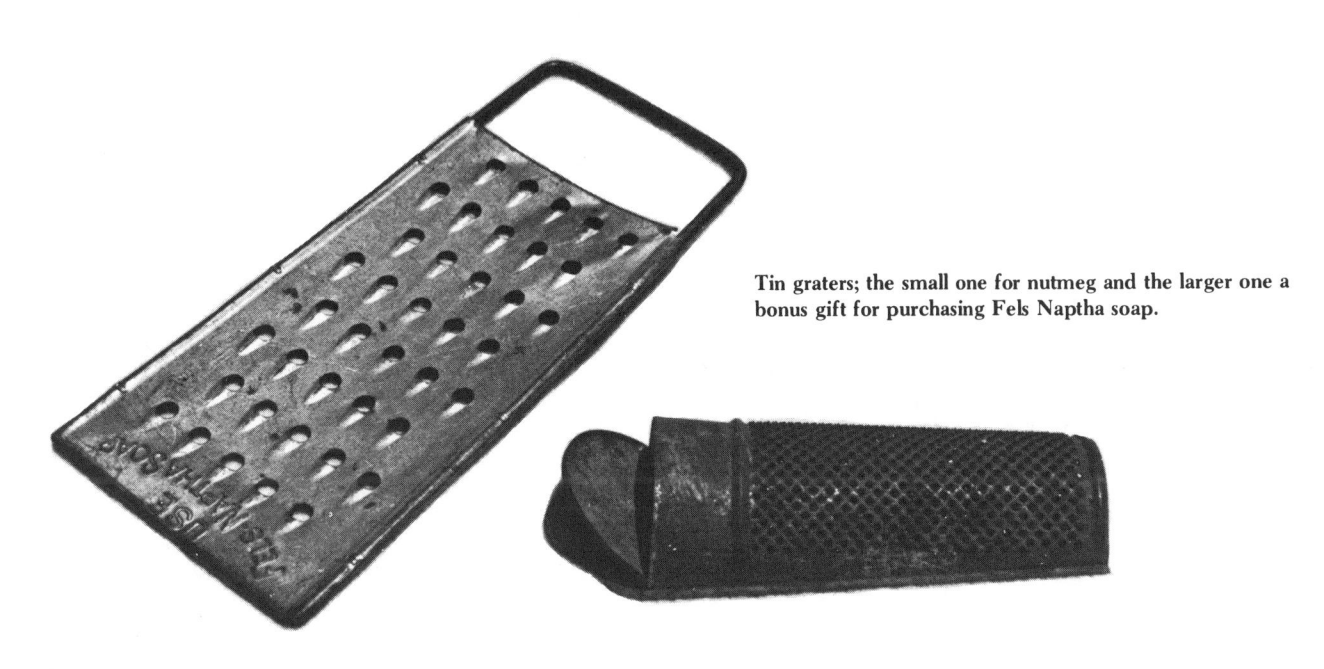

Tin graters; the small one for nutmeg and the larger one a bonus gift for purchasing Fels Naptha soap.

Gingersnaps

Cream one cup of shortening and two cups of dark brown sugar smoothly. Blend in one cup of molasses and one beaten egg. Sift four cups of flour, a half teaspoon of salt, two teaspoons of baking soda and two teaspoons of ginger into the creamed mixture and stir, adding one teaspoon of vanilla flavoring and one teaspoon of lemon extract. Chill the mixture until it is easily handled.

Shape the dough in small balls and place on a greased cookie sheet and bake in a moderate oven for about a quarter of an hour. (These gingersnaps went very well with a glass of cider—both have a special *zing* to them!)

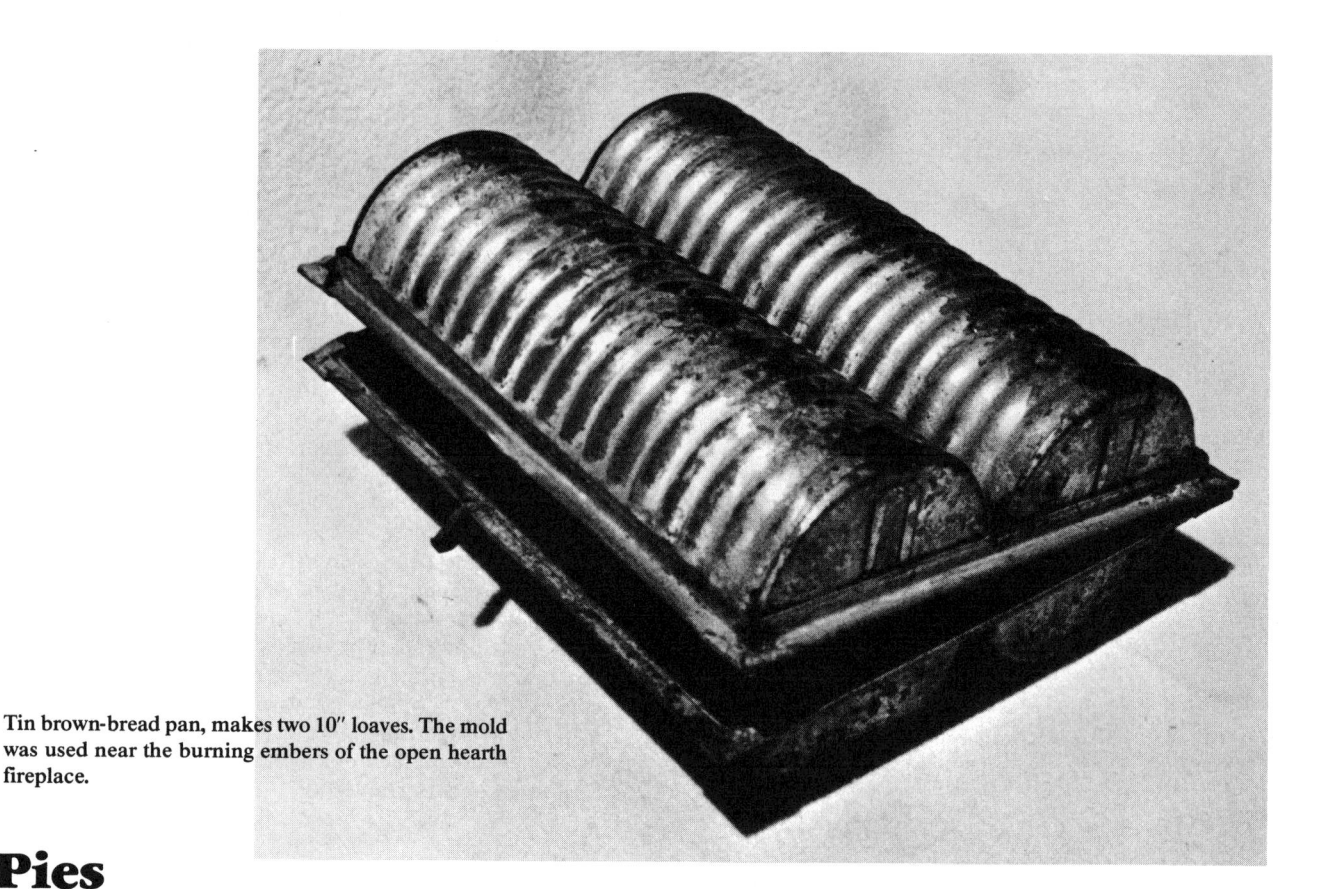

Tin brown-bread pan, makes two 10" loaves. The mold was used near the burning embers of the open hearth fireplace.

Pies

Almond Pie

Blanch the skins from a quarter pound of shelled almonds by pouring scalding water over them. Pound the almonds in a mortar to a fine paste. Stir together a quarter pound of butter with a quarter pound of powdered sugar and add two tablespoons of brandy.

Beat the whites of six eggs until they stand alone, stir the almond paste and whites of eggs, alternating by adding the butter-sugar mixture and blend well. Pour the mixture on a puff-paste lining, and as one old recipe noted, "trim and notch it"—meaning the pie crust rollers illustrated on page 26 should be used. Bake in a moderate oven for half an hour. (This was a show-off dessert, not commonly made for everyday appetites and occasions, certainly not served to the harvest hands!)

Raspberry Raisin Pie

Boil one and a half cups of raisins in one and a half cups of raspberry juice (the sweetened juice is often left over from home canning but juice from canned or frozen berries may be used). Blend one and a half tablespoons of cornstarch and four tablespoons of cold raspberry juice and add it to the heating raisins, stirring constantly until it is clear and thick. Pour into pastry-lined pie plates and cover with a crust. Bake at 400° for a half hour.

(This doesn't have a single berry in it yet it fools almost everyone—it is sometimes called "Mock raspberry" and the word "raisin" is somehow deemphasized perhaps because the raisin was in most pantries whereas the raspberry was seasonal and often scarce and expensive—so the juice was used effectively!)

Maple Nut Pie

Combine two cups of milk and one cup of maple sugar in the top of a double boiler and heat to dissolve the sugar. In a quarter cup of cold milk mix in three tablespoons of cornstarch and blend into the heating mixture stirring until it thickens. Remove from heat and blend in three beaten egg yolks and return it to the heat and beat until smooth for three minutes. Remove from heat and add one tablespoon of butter, one and a half teaspoons of vanilla extract and salt. Pour into baked pastry shells then sprinkle three-fourths of a cup of finely chopped walnuts over the top.

Beat together three tablespoons of sugar and the whites of three eggs until stiff and cover the pie. Bake in a moderate oven until the meringue is light brown.

(Maple sugar was once a common sweetener, now it is scarce and very expensive. Brown sugar or molasses could be used as a substitute. Black walnuts were used as a topping because they too were easily available for the gathering and "picking," but now these too are quite expensive, so this once thrifty pie would be very expensive to make today if the original recipe was followed and the ingredients had to be purchased.)

White Potato Pie

Mash a boiled potato, add a half cup of sugar and a large spoonful of butter and whip into a creamy mixture. Add the yolks of two eggs, a half cup of milk and the grated rind and juice of one half lemon or orange. Stir in the beaten whites of two eggs. Bake in a crust lined pie plate until the top is a golden brown. (Those who partake of this pie for the first time will seldom, if ever, guess what the basic ingredient is!)

Country Pantry Pie

In an unbaked crust lined pie plate, sprinkle four tablespoons of brown sugar; small specks of butter and sprinkle one tablespoon of flour. Pour in a cup and a quarter of milk, sprinkle cinnamon on top and bake in a moderate oven until the mixture is thick and firm.

(This has been referred to by various labels but the ingredients were common to every pantry. If brown sugar was not available some used molasses or maple sugar; if cinnamon was out of stock, nutmeg was sprinkled on top instead, and if they were out of butter it meant milk the cow and churning the cream!)

Prune Pie

Soak a half-pound of dried prunes overnight and cook slowly until tender. Mix together a half cup of the prune juice, a quarter cup of sugar; three-fourths cup of molasses and the beaten yolks of four eggs.

Cut the prunes into small pieces, mix in a quarter cup of preserves (any of the following will do: grape, peach, plum or apple) and add a quarter cup of melted butter and one teaspoon of lemon juice or vinegar. Add the two mixtures together and stir well, place them in a pastry-lined pan and bake at a moderate temperature until firm.

Green Tomato Mince Meat

Cut one peck of green tomatoes into small pieces and cook for three hours. Slice three lemons and one orange and remove the pits; add two pounds of seedless raisins and five pounds of sugar; add one cup of cider vinegar and one teaspoon each of cloves, nutmeg and cinnamon add these ingredients and cook for an additional hour. (Some folks add grated orange peel, minced citron and apple butter in small quantities to create a heavier body).

Pour in preserving jars and seal. This is an old fashioned mince meat substitute that was made during the season when tomatoes were plentiful and grown in the home garden. Like much of the farm activities, the work came long before the pleasure of the warm mince meat pie on a crisp fall day.

Butter Scotch Pie

Heat one cup of brown sugar with two heaping tablespoons of butter until soft. Stir in one egg yolk, a cup of milk and gradually add two heaping teaspoons of flour and beat until smooth and thick. Add vanilla or almond extract to taste and pour into a baked pie crust. Beat the white of one egg adding a tablespoon of sugar and spread it over the mixture and brown in the oven.

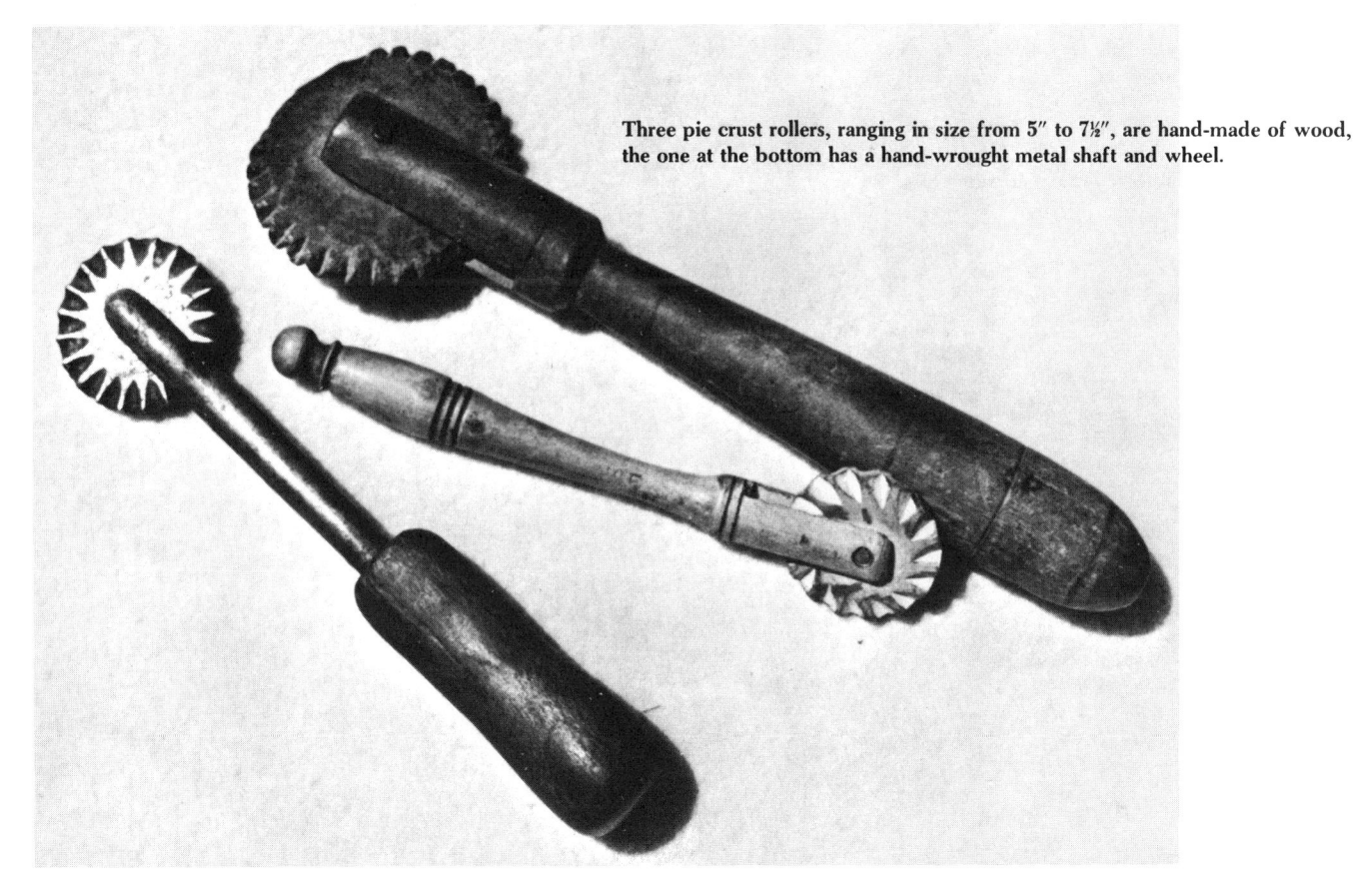

Three pie crust rollers, ranging in size from 5″ to 7½″, are hand-made of wood, the one at the bottom has a hand-wrought metal shaft and wheel.

Cranberry Pie

Chop a half cup of cranberries; a half cup of raisins and mix with a half cup of sugar and a half cup of cold water. Boil the mixture and add a tablespoon of flour and a teaspoon of vanilla or almond extract. Pour the cooked mixture into a pastry lined pie plate.

(The cranberry is commonly found in collections of New England recipes, yet these tasty, tart berries were widely used elsewhere. It was quite often used as a replacement for the strawberry in the fall season. In some sections of Pennsylvania the recipe noted above was called "mock cherry pie" and in New Jersey there was a practice of using cranberries for a cake referred to as "mock strawberry short cake." Nevertheless, the cranberry has a place in its own right and doesn't need to be an imitation for cherries, strawberries, raspberries or anything else!)

Peach Snitz Pie

Soak three cups of dried peaches in water for several hours. Drain and add one cup of peach juice, a cup of sugar, several dashes of nutmeg and salt and bring this mixture to a boil. Blend together two tablespoons of cold water and two tablespoons of cornstarch and add to the hot peach concoction stirring continually for three to four minutes.

Add three tablespoons of butter and a teaspoon of lemon extract. Cool, then pour into a pastry lined pie pan. Cover the top with a pastry and slash with a sharp knife or pierce with a three-pronged fork. Bake in a hot oven for 25 minutes or until the crust is golden brown.

(Apples and peaches were often preserved by drying in the sun; obviously during the summer months fresh fruit pies were baked but during the winter months the so-called snitz pies were popular.)

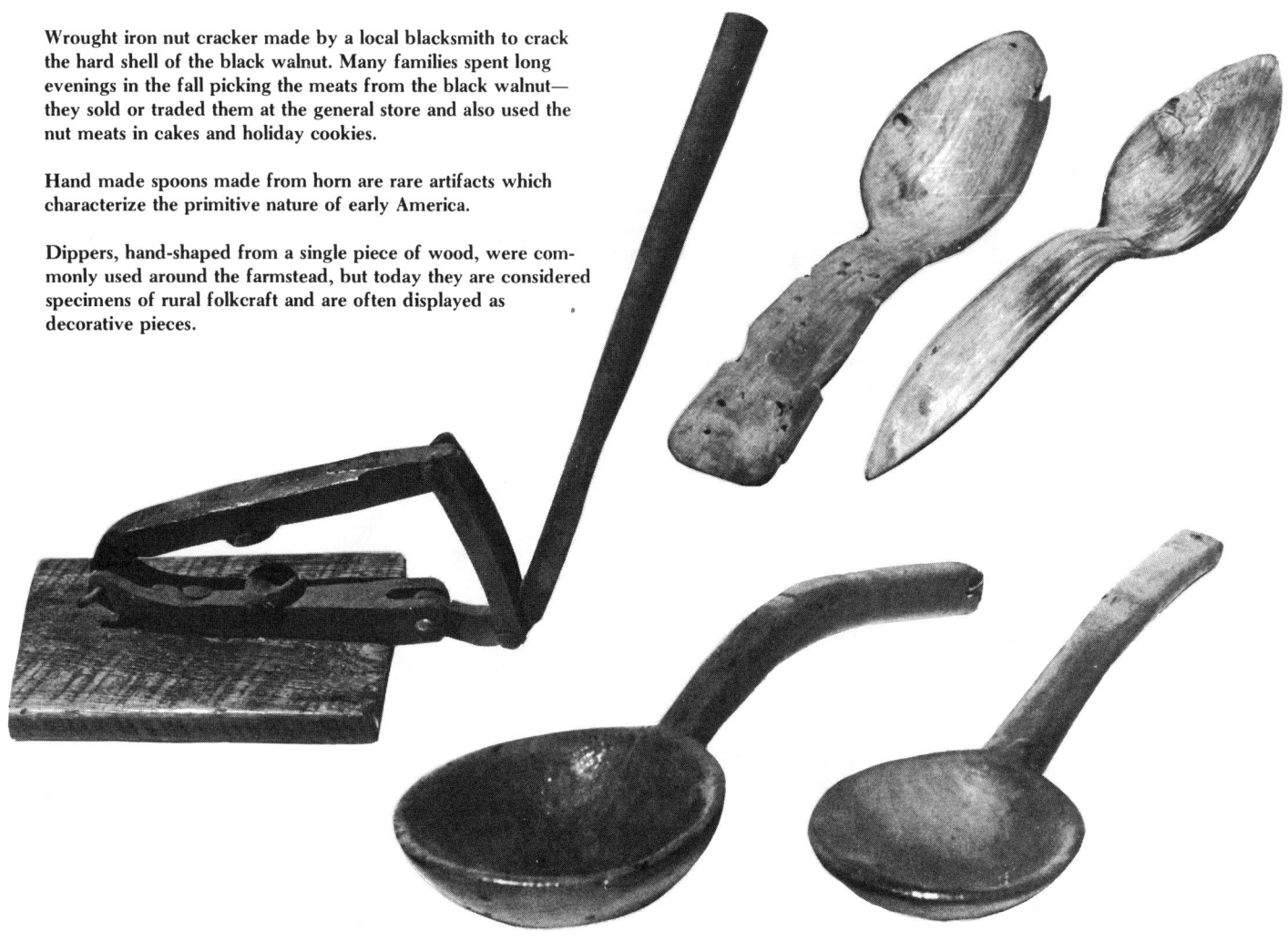

Wrought iron nut cracker made by a local blacksmith to crack the hard shell of the black walnut. Many families spent long evenings in the fall picking the meats from the black walnut—they sold or traded them at the general store and also used the nut meats in cakes and holiday cookies.

Hand made spoons made from horn are rare artifacts which characterize the primitive nature of early America.

Dippers, hand-shaped from a single piece of wood, were commonly used around the farmstead, but today they are considered specimens of rural folkcraft and are often displayed as decorative pieces.

Beverages

A century and more ago beverages were made on the farmstead in a wide variety of forms and types, well beyond the hot coffee, tea and chocolate or the summer lemonades commonly consumed and created at home today.

Cider was cheap and plentiful and therefore the most popular drink of the people. Distilled cider, in the form of apple brandy and Apple Jack, was a leading "hard" drink.

The wide spread apple orchards provided an abundance of the fruit, so apples were included in many other early mixed drinks, such as *Beverige* (made of a mixture of cider, water and spices) and in some *syllabub* concoctions, such as the famous Colonial New England Judge Sewall's recipe:

Sewall's Syllabub

"Fill your sillabub pot with syder and a good store of sugar and a little nutmeg, stir it wel together, put in as much thick cream—two or three spoonsful at a time . . . then stir it together . . . let it stand two hours at least."

In more contemporary times, this writer attained an early-in life "dizzy spell" from consistently sipping from a jug believed to be apple cider. It turned out to be "Jersey Lightning"! From that same central New Jersey area the famous Laird's distillery made Apple Jack since the early days.

Today, apple cider or apple jack is used in numerous mixed drinks such as Jack Rose, Jersey Libra, Apple Knocker, Calamity Jane Collins, Roaring 20's and others. Little wonder the Temperance movement included cider on its list of prohibited beverages!

Beverages were available at almost every type of social occasion ranging from funerals to weddings and festive holidays to hard working days such as harvesting, corn husking, house and barn raisings.

When cider was unavailable in summer months because it turned or the supply was depleted, beer became a popular beverage. Home-brewed from assorted ingredients including ginger, spruce, molasses and even persimmons, beer brewing gave evidence to our Yankee ingenuity.

Those earlier days of self-sufficiency brought some interesting beverages with unique names such as *Switchel, Summer Beverige* (a mixture of molasses, ginger and water), *Perry* (a concoction made from pears), *Peachy* (obviously created from peaches), *Metheglin* (an ancient intoxicating drink made from honey, water and yeast), as well as *Punch, Shrub,* and *Flip*.

Coffee, chocolate, and tea were popular drinks, but at times so very expensive that other beverages replaced them. In early America thrift and self-sufficiency dominated and economy meant "economizing" so men adapted to their means, including adopting ingeniously to the available resources.

Ironing was a hot and heavy chore—there were irons of almost every size and shape, but most were heavy, inconvenient, and called for heating on the kitchen stove. The handles of the all-iron varieties conducted heat and became almost unbearable to handle. Illustrated are two typical hand irons and a sad iron waxer.

Tomato Wine

Press the juice from enough ripe tomatoes to make a gallon and add four pounds of dark brown sugar and let the liquid stand overnight. The next day, drain the mixture through a cheese cloth and remove the pulp. Allow the wine to stand for two or three months then draw off into bottles. (Although tomato wine was a fermented intoxicating beverage, it was somehow thought of as a tonic or as "medicinal" by the Temperance folks. Furthermore, it is said that even heavy drinkers who overconsumed tomato would not get the "snakes.")

Walnut Wine

Boil together one gallon of water and three or four pounds of honey for an hour. Pour the boiling liquid over two or three dozen walnut leaves and let it stand overnight. Remove the leaves, add a teaspoon of yeast and let it work for three days. Pour the mixture into a crock and let it remain in a cool place for three months. Bottle it. (This drink is a beverage once classified as in the *Mead* category using honey as a basic ingredient.)

Potato Wine

Prepare a half bushel of potatoes (that have been frosted or have become soft and watery) by pounding them with a wooden mallet or by pressing them in an apple press. Add five gallons of water and boil for an hour with a quarter pound of hops and a quarter pound of white ginger. Add yeast and allow the mixture to stand for three days. Draw off the liquid and add a half pound of sugar for every gallon of potato wine. After three months it will be ready. (It is said that if you drink enough potato wine you get to "see your great-great grandfather"!)

Mixed Fruit Wine

Combine in approximately equal quantities; red, black and white currants; cherries and raspberries and crush them well before adding one gallon of water for each four pounds of fruit. Add three pounds of sugar for each gallon of liquid and allow it to stand overnight. Press and strain through a cheese or flannel cloth and allow this mixture to stand three days, stirring regularly and removing the froth that rises to the top. Let it work for another three days then add one cup of brandy for each gallon of wine and place it in a barrel or container and seal it. In two years it will be a rich potent drink.

Coffee mill, with pewter grinder and of walnut wood. Right is wooden nutmeg grinder.

Wooden scoop with simple carved decoration is from New England. Measures 12" long.

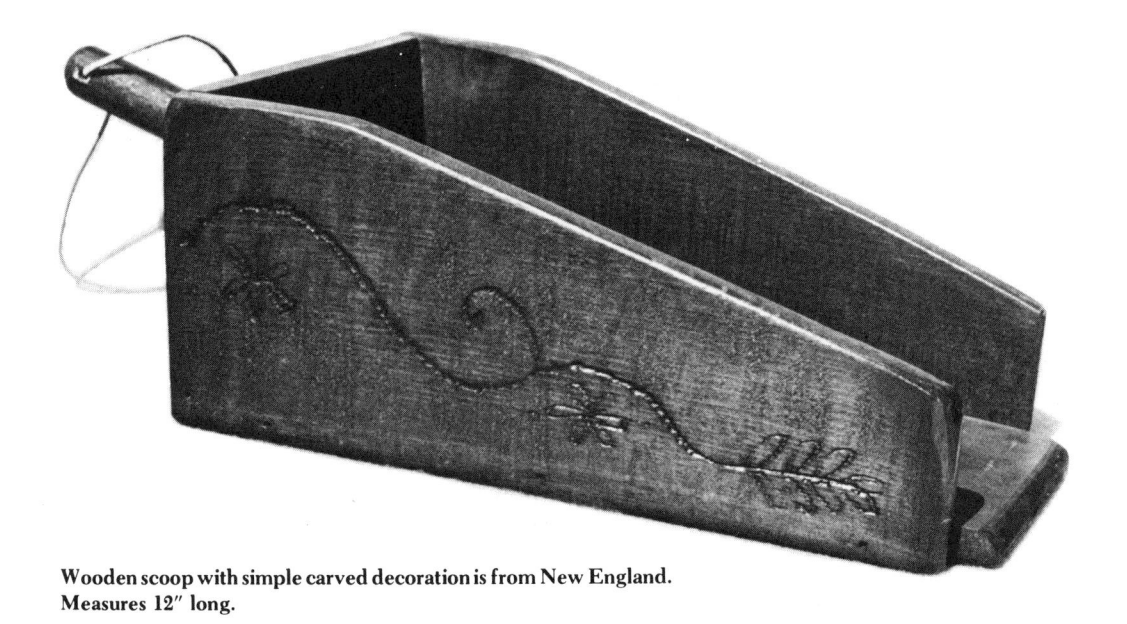

Blackberry Wine

Add one quart of boiling water for each gallon of blackberries. The berries should be crushed and well pressed after they are measured. Let the ingredients stand a full twenty-four hours before straining. Add two pounds of sugar for each gallon of liquid, bottle, cork and be patient for a year. (Blackberry wine has been a traditional folk medicine for stomach aches and upsets of the intestines. Some old-timers drank some every morning to prevent such complaints!)

Flaxseed Tea

Pour one quart of boiling water over four tablespoonfuls of whole flaxseed and allow it to steep for four hours. Strain out the seeds and add the juice of two lemons and sugar to taste. If it is too thick, add more water. (This was a medicinal tea which was soothing for colds and fever. Mother made all her children take this in the Spring, healthy as we might have been, because she claimed it "thinned" our blood which had "thickened" during the cold winter months!)

White Spruce Beer

Boil five gallons of water and add three pounds of sugar, two ounces of essence of spruce and a half ounce of yeast and continue boiling for an hour. Keep the liquid in a moderately warm place for forty-eight hours, stirring from time to time. Place the mixture in a crock or barrel skimming off any surface scum that accumulates. After four days transfer the liquid into pint bottles. (Other popular non-fermented and non-intoxicating beverages were made from citrus and other fruits. Nevertheless, chocolate and coffee were perhaps the most popular beverages while tea was the most economically provided leaves from native plants were dried and used—peppermint and spearmint were unusually popular.)

Maple Beer

Boil a gallon of water, add two cups of maple syrup and a half teaspoon of nutmeg. When the concoction is luke warm add a teaspoon of yeast and allow the liquid to ferment. Then bottle it and it will be ready in four or five days.

Spiced Cocoa

Combine a half cup of sugar and a half cup of cocoa in a cup of boiling water with twelve whole cloves and a dash of salt and heat in the top of a double boiler. Add five cups of milk and a half teaspoon of vanilla extract and stir briskly.

Serve in mugs with a long cinnamon stick which can be used as a muddler. (This has a unique taste and young folks considered it a special treat! Heck, we old folks liked it too!)

Wassail—All Family Style

The Christmas season was a family affair on the farms of America. It was a festive occasion shared by young and old alike, yet it was a family fellowship when the common bond was reaffirmed. Our Old-World heritage was perpetuated in many of the season customs and traditions, the English wassail (which was made of spiced ale or wine and baked apples) became part of the American Twelfth day practices, but with modifications because our celebration focuses on all the family so the wassail recipe that follows was non-alcoholic.

Combine together 3 cups of apple cider; 1 cup of pineapple juice; 1½ cups of orange juice, ½ cup of grapefruit juice; ½ cup of lemon juice and a half cup of sugar. Heat the liquid and add two sticks of cinnamon. Make a spice bag of cheesecloth and insert 1½ teaspoons of whole allspice and ½ teaspoon of whole cloves and place the sack in the liquid. Allow the mixture to come to a boil, then let it simmer for a half hour. Peel oranges into slices and stud them with whole cloves and place them in the punch bowl. Remove the spice bag and pour the hot punch over the oranges and they will float! This should make a dozen servings.

An alcoholic punch can be made by simply adding wine to taste while the liquid simmers.

Fruits

Apples and Onions

Melt fat in a large fry pan. Add three cups of sliced onions and three cups of diced apples and cook over slow heat until tender. Add two tablespoons of sugar and salt and pepper to taste. It is perhaps best cooked in bacon or sausage fat, this gives the apples a good flavor; others use brown sugar and add a dash of nutmeg. (This may appear a strange mixture, when you recollect the saying "An apple a day keeps the doctor away and an onion a day keeps everyone away!")

Apple Snow

Grate two cups of raw apples, add a quarter cup of lemon juice and sprinkle heavily with ground nutmeg and a dash of salt. Add two tablespoons of sugar and allow the mixture to chill. Beat the whites of two eggs until they stand stiff, gradually beat in four tablespoons of sugar and fold this into the chilled apple mixture. Serve in sherbert glasses or dessert dishes, some prefer to dress it up with a light sprinkling of grated chocolate or red/green sugar used to decorate cookies. (This is delicious yet easily and speedily made and with the eye-appeal which gives the impression of something very special!)

Dried Chestnuts and Corn

Chestnuts were gathered in the fall of the year, shelled as soon as they were gathered, dried and stored for winter use. A combination of dried corn and dried chestnuts—in equal quantities was excellent. (Soak chestnuts in cold water overnight.)

Fried Green Tomatoes

Slice tomatoes about a quarter of an inch thick. Salt them and let them stand for a half hour, dredge in flour seasoned with salt and pepper and fry in bacon fat until browned on both sides. (Tomato slices are also good dredged in beaten egg and cracker crumbs!)

Baked Maple Apples

Core eight medium-sized apples and place them in a buttered baking dish. Add a tablespoon of water and pour a half cup of maple syrup over the apples. Fill the space where the core was removed with raisins and chopped nuts and add a sprinkling of nutmeg or cinnamon over the apples. Bake in a medium oven until tender. Serve hot or cold, with or without cream or milk.

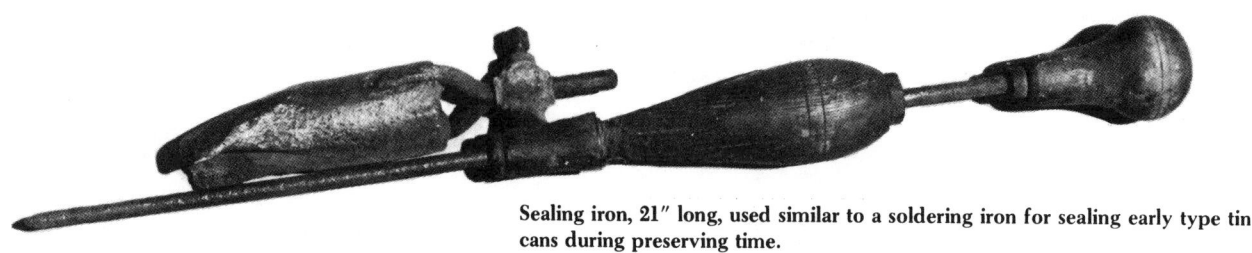

Sealing iron, 21" long, used similar to a soldering iron for sealing early type tin cans during preserving time.

Cooking

In 1914 a city school mar'm visited Clear Spring Farm for the summer and was fascinated by what she observed in the kitchen. The cooking, baking, and preserving involved a wide-range of dishes and the procedures seemed never-ending, although carried out without haste in a casual, seemingly simple manner.

While breakfast was being prepared, bread, cake, pie or a pudding was in the oven to be available for the noon or evening meal—the wood stove was used efficiently.

The observer noted that stale bread was never wasted: it was heated in the oven, rolled and made into bread-crumbs for future use; cut into cubes to be served with soup as croutons; sliced and heated as toast; covered with creamed chipped beef and served for lunch; made into a bread pudding as a dessert; or in many other ways, but never wasted!

Vegetables were also used to the fullest extent. The outer leaves of lettuce were chopped fine into the salad; the heart was soaked with vinegar and chopped fine into a salad; celery tips were chopped and added to soup stock, and celery leaves were dried and crushed for use as a flavoring. Most vegetables were assumed to be available as additions to soup stock—peelings were given to the chickens!

Even bacon fat or ham grease was used. Heated it became the basis for hot German salad dressing, and in other ways it added a touch of flavor to heated foods.

Strangely, the city school mar'm did not notice that many of the ingredients commonly thrown away in the city had been added to the dishes and foods she thought were so wholesome, tasty and nutritious out on the farm!

The Monday Blues

The common expression, "the Monday blues," may have been the result of the recurring task of doing the family wash, which was almost exclusively done on Monday.

This time-consuming, laborious chore centered in the kitchen at the cast-iron wood stove where water was heated in huge copper boilers (nor were there any dials, gadgets or faucets to turn on or off, only a hand pump to fill the buckets). Washing was done over a tub in which a scrubbing board was placed—some fortunate folks had a wooden "automatic" human-powered washer that was at least a back-saving device. When the wash was scrubbed, boiled and rinsed, out came the wash baskets, clothes lines and poles for the drying procedure. When the laundry was dry there was the ironing . . . little wonder the Monday blues!

Some of the later type hand irons had wooden handles (left, Colebrookdale Iron Co., Doylestown, Penna.) and the "modern" one at the right had a heat shield and was called "The Monitor."

Dunking

A favorite aunt was an avowed "dunker," she enjoyed dipping toast in tea and doughnuts in coffee—but not without mental reservations. She finally resolved doubts about the social propriety by rationalizing that dipping rapidly wasn't the same as dunking—so she went on enjoying her dipping and dunking for the remainder of her days.

Dunking can be a noble art, it cannot by any stretch of the imagination be a major social fault, so dunk a doughnut anytime and anyplace and at any angle!

The Applebutter Boiling

Applebutter boiling was an autumn neighborhood folk gathering at which old and young intermingled, combining fun, fellowship and purpose.

Bushels of apples were pared, quartered, and cored. Meanwhile, cider was being boiled down in a large copper kettle ranging from 20 to 40 gallons in size over an outdoor wood fire.

When the cider was boiled down to about half its original quantity the apples were added and the mixture constantly stirred. Because of the heat and the large kettle, long handled goose-neck paddles were used. These were often manned by a couple—perhaps a flirting male and female—whose task was to make sure the pulp did not stick to the sides of the kettle and burn or scorch the entire batch. The best way to move the handle in stirring was the subject of an old verse:

"Twice around then once down the middle,
That's the way to stir the applebutter kittle."

Obviously, while the applebutter was being stirred, there was little other work for the folks at the gathering except to tend the fire—so it was fun and games.

When the mixture reached a thick pudding-like texture, cinnamon, ground cloves and allspice were added, and finally the butter was poured into pottery crocks for storage.

Applebutter boilings were held in Pennsylvania, Maryland, West Virginia, Ohio, Virginia and elsewhere. Smaller quantities of peach butter and pear butter were also commonly made but generally without the festivities of a frolic.

Ingenious apple butter stirrer. Hand-made to fit on a large copper kettle. With hand-made wooden cog gears that turn the paddle, the three pieces when joined together with wooden pegs provide an 86" long turning crank type handle! Most folks just used the long handled paddles.

Baking

A city school mar'm noted that Aunt Sarah baked a wide variety of cakes without any reference to notes or cook books. During that summer of 1914 Aunt Sarah baked loaf cakes, layer cakes, cup cakes and cake squares. They were chocolate, vanilla, and marble, lemon, nut, and even fruit cakes, with a wide assortment of icings and fillings. Yet, there was a secret—a single recipe was basic to all of them!

Aunt Sarah's Basic Cake

Cream together one and a quarter cups of granulated sugar with a half cup of butter or lard. Add two cups of flour and two teaspoons of baking powder. Mix in three eggs; a half cup of milk and one teaspoon of vanilla. (This batter can be used as a layer cake, or baked in square cake pans and served in squares, in muffin pans and baked as cup cakes, in loaf pans and served sliced as pound cake. The batter can be simply modified by

(1) adding one cup of chopped nut meats
(2) adding two tablespoons of unsweetened melted chocolate, for a chocolate layer cake.
(3) Adding chocolate to half the batter and mix alternately in pans to have a marble cake.
(4) Adding shaved citron and lemon flavoring for a lemon cake.
(5) adding a teaspoon of cinnamon, ginger and a dash of nutmeg and cloves; a cup of raisins or dried currants. Bake in a loaf pan and you have a fruit cake.

What the school mar'm really observed was not the application of an unusually good memory based on years of experience, but instead the simple old time use of common sense!

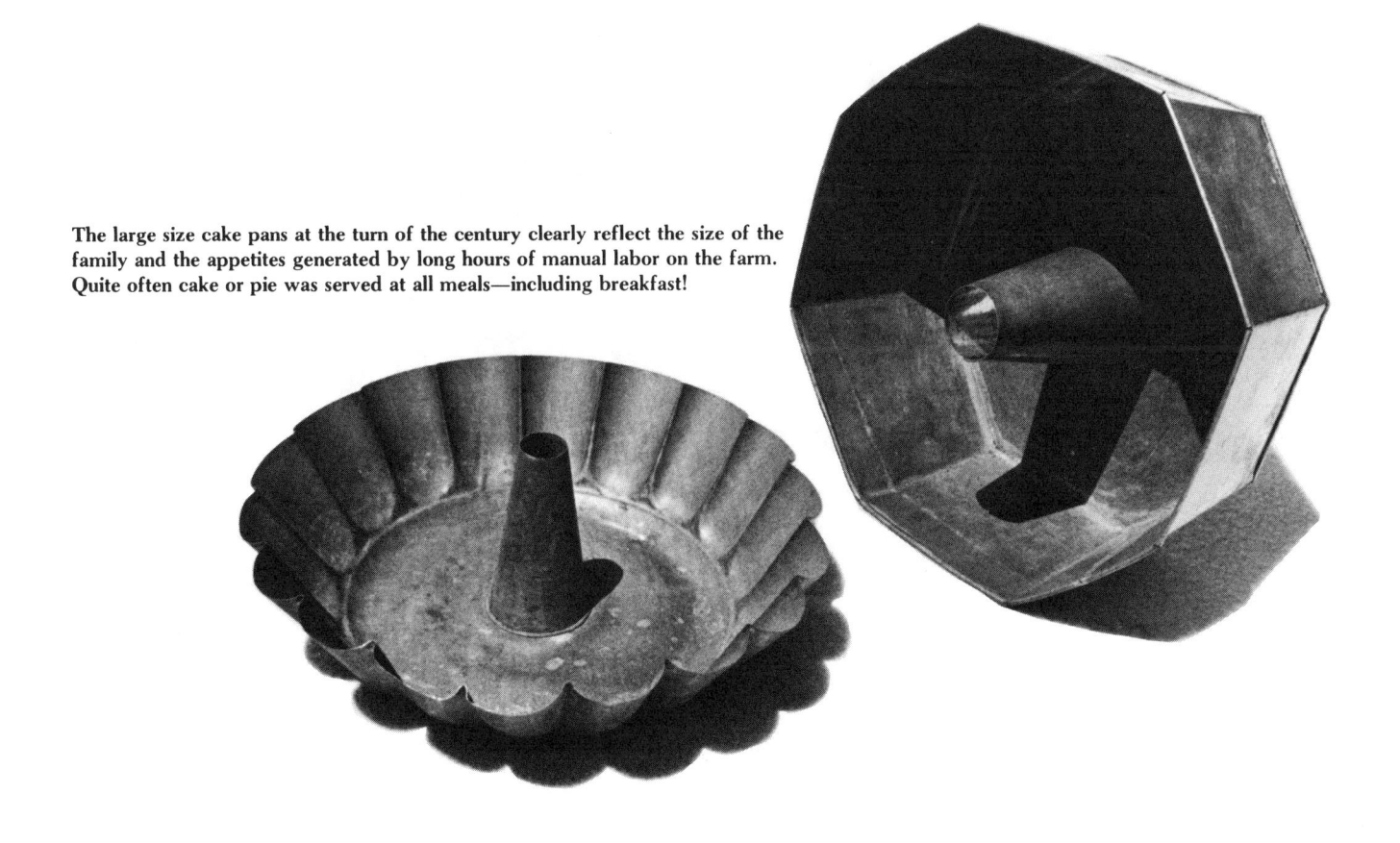

The large size cake pans at the turn of the century clearly reflect the size of the family and the appetites generated by long hours of manual labor on the farm. Quite often cake or pie was served at all meals—including breakfast!

Gathering

Having been hospitalized for some three months without meaningful improvement in strength and health, a friend confided that what was needed was "a mess of spring greens!"

She was one of a passing generation of countryfolk reared to the notion that the early spring dandelion does wonders for what ails you. Some claim it is good for aches, pains, sluggishness, and simple spring fever while others view it as a good luck dish and insist it *must* be eaten on Maundy Thursday to insure good health the year through. Others simply say it tastes good!

While the suburbanite spends hours weeding the plant from his lawn for appearance sake, some of his country cousins gather the tender leaves for table use. (Some of the country males gather the plants and process it into a potent beverage for both medicinal and social usage!)

Kidney shaped basket, hand-woven in Pendleton county, West Virginia. A type commonly used to gather eggs from the hen house nests. Measuring 13" across the handle.

Butchering

In earlier times it was claimed that every part of a hog was useable except the squeal. Perhaps only a small exaggeration, but the hog did provide the luscious loin of pork, hams, pork chops, bacon, side meat, sausage and a variety of local and regional specialties such as scrapple. Pork was the mainstay of the farm family's winter diet, and at butchering time little was wasted.

The hooves were made into pickled pig's feet; the head into jelly-like souse or scrapple, the entrails were scraped and used for stuffing sausage meat, and the stomach casing was also used for stuffing. The fat was either rendered into lard or used for boiling into soap. Some families kept the bristles and sold them for use in plastering or making brushes. Others made a salve from the gall bladder which has been acclaimed as unusually helpful in cases of frost bite!

Butchering day was an important and busy day on the farm! Family members were awakened an hour before the customary time and given specific tasks; big iron kettles were hung over the outdoor fireplace; a trough was set up and fires started under them; bucket after bucket of water was hand-pumped from the well and poured into the trough; butchering tools were gathered and when all preparations were ready —the trip to the pig sty!

The hog carcass was hauled to the scalding trough and placed in the hot water, then scraped clean of bristles and hung on a tall wooden tripod, hind feet up. The butchering followed, a task usually assigned to the men while the women worked on finished products such as cutting fat into cubes for rendering into lard; grinding meat into sausage; boiling the juices and meat, preparing the puddings, and making pans of scrapple or panhaus.

Butchering day was a busy day, but there was time for gossip, humor, jokes and pranks and at day's end there was usually a tasty feast—but it was always work before pleasure!

Extra-large sized iron sausage stuffer, measuring 28". Patented in 1858.

Index

Almond Pie 20
Applebutter 14
Apple
  Johnny Pudding 16
  Stuffing 7
Asparagus Soup 2
Aunt Sarah's Basic Cake 29

Bacon
  Dressing, Hot 6
  —Liverwurst Sandwich 13
  —Peanut Butter Sandwich 13
Banana Fritters 8
Beans
  Baked 9
  Sandwich 13
Beef
  Corned, Red Flannel Hash 5
Beet Greens 9
Beverages 23
Biscuits 11
Blackberry Wine 25
Bran Bread 12
Breads 10
  see also Biscuits,
  Buns, Doughnuts,
  Gingerbread, Muffins,
  Pudding, Stuffing
Buttermilk Doughnuts 10
Butterscotch Pie 21

Cake 17, 29
Cake Toppings 18
Cheese
  and Bread (Egg Dish) 14
  —Egg Sandwich 13
  —Potato Fritter 8
  Soup 2
Chicken
  Croquettes 5
  —Potato Puffs 9
Chipped Meat Sandwich 13
Cinnamon Loaf 12
Clove Cake 17

Cocoa, Spiced 25
Codfish Cakes 4
Cookies 19
Corn
  Chowder 3
  Fritters 8
  —meal, Indian Pudding 15
  Mush, Fried 10
Cornbread Stuffing 7
Country Pantry Pie 21
Cranberry
  Muffins 10
  Pie 22
Cruellers 11
Cucumber-Chive Sandwich 13

Doughnuts 10
Dressing
  Salad 6
  see also Stuffing

Eggs
  —Cheese Sandwich 13
  "Cheese and bread" 14
  Farmers Winter Omelet 5
Eggplant Fritters 8

Farmers Winter Omelet 5
Fish
  Codfish Cakes 4
Flaxseed Tea 25
Fritters 8
Fruit, Mixed Wine 24

Gingerbread 17
Ginger Cake 17
Gingersnaps 19
Green Pea Soup, Fresh 3

Honey Frosting 18
Hot Dressing, for Salads 6
Huckleberry Muffins 10

Indian Pudding 15

Lemon Dressing 6
  —Sauce 18
Lentil Soup 2
Liver
  Loaf 4
  —Wurst Sandwich 13

Maple
  Nut Icing 18
  Pie 20
  Beer 25
Maryland Beaten Biscuits 11
Milk Biscuits 11
Mocha Icing 18
Muffins 10
Mush 10
Mustard Dressing 6

New England Boiled Dinner 2
Nutmeg Sauce
  Sauce 6
  Wafers 19

Omelet 5
Onion
  Greens 9
  —Cheese Sandwich 13
Orange Stuffing
  Stuffing 7
  Peel, Candied 14
Oyster Stuffing 7

Parsnips, Deep Fried 9
Peace
  Fritters 8
  Pudding 15
  Snitz Pie 22
Peanut
  Muffins 10
  Butter-Bacon Sandwich 13
Philadelphia Pepper Pot 3
Pies 20
Pork
  Stove-top Supper 4
Potato
  —Cheese Cakes 9
  —Onion Cakes 9

Pie 20
Scalloped 9
Sweet Pudding 16
Wine 24
Prune Pie 21
Puddings 15

Raisin
  Drop Cookies 19
  Jam 14
  —Raspberry Pie 20
  —Rice Pudding 16
Raspberry-Raisin Pie 20
Red Flannel Hash 5
Rhubarb Marmalade 14
Rice-Meat Pie 4

Sage Stuffing 7
Salad Dressing 6
Sandwiches 13
Sauces 6
Sausage Stuffing 7
Shepherd's Pie 4
Spinach Soup 2
Squash Cake 17
Stove-top Supper 4
Stuffing 7
Sweet Dough 12
Syllabub 23

Tea 25
Tomato
  Green Mincemeat 21
  Wine 24
Tripe
  Philadelphia Pepper Pot 3

Vegetables 9

Wafers 19
Walnut Wine 24
Wassail 25
White Sauce 6
White Spruce Beer 25
Whole Wheat Bread 12

Index to Antiques

Applebutter Stirrer 28

Baskets 5, 30
Bread Pan 20

Cabbage Cutter 11
Cake Pans 29
Candle Box 12
Cheese Grater 18
Coffee Mill 24

Dippers 22

Food Press 9

Grinder 17, 24

Huckleberry Picker 16

Irons 23, 27
Ironware 22, 26, 27, 31

Lard Press 7, 8

Molds 13
Mortar and Pestle 4

Nutcracker 21
Nutmeg Grinder 24

Pie Crust Rollers 21

Sausage Stuffer 31
Scoop 25
Sealing Iron 26
Spoons 22
Sugar Chest 15

Tinware 3, 13, 14, 19, 20, 29

Water Bucket 14
Water Dipper, tin 14
Wood 9, 11, 12, 15, 21, 25, 28